TALL & SMALL

A Book about Height

by
Kate Gilbert Phifer

Illustrations by
Dennis Kendrick

Walker and Company

New York, New York

First published in the United States of America in 1987 by the Walker Publishing Company, Inc.

Published simultaneously in Canada by John Wiley & Sons Canada, Limited, Rexdale, Ontario.

Library of Congress Cataloging-in-Publication Data

Phifer, Kate Gilbert, 1937-
    Tall & small.

    Includes index.
    Summary: Discusses the feelings and problems caused by one's height, particularly at the preteen stage, the factors involved in growth, and ways to feel good about one's height—whatever it is.
    1. Stature, Short—Psychological aspects—Juvenile literature.   Stature, Tall—Psychological aspects—Juvenile literature.   [1. Size.   2. Growth]   I. Kendrick, Dennis, ill.   II. Title.   III. Title: Tall and small.
QP84.P54   1987   612'.6   86-32401

ISBN 0-8027-6684-6
ISBN 0-8027-6685-4 (lib. bdg.)

Printed in the United States of America

10 9 8 7 6 5 4 3 2 1

Book design by Laurie McBarnette

Contents

For the Creator, who made us all . . . tall and small

". . . Do not look at his appearance or
at the height of his stature, . . . for
God sees not as man sees, for man looks
at the outward appearance, but the Lord
looks at the heart."

1 Samuel 16:7

INTRODUCTION

I've been short since birth. Through childhood and adolescence I grew slowly, and then I stopped growing at age fourteen. A good friend said she'd give me a big party when I reached five feet, but I never made it. I'm four feet nine inches tall.

How tall are you?

Height is a unique feature of your body, because instead of seeing it, you feel it. You see your hair when you brush it, your arms and legs when you wash or dress. It's easy to look in the mirror at your face. But do you really notice your height—even in a full-length mirror?

You feel your height by comparing yourself to other people, your family and friends. You feel how tall or small you are by comparing yourself to things around you—kitchen cupboards, bathroom mirrors, bicycles, or chairs. If you feel comfortable with your height, you rarely notice it. But at one time or other most people feel they are too tall or too short, and this feeling can be embarrassing, frustrating, and even painful.

The time when being short was the hardest for me was during sixth, seventh, and eighth grades. No matter what makes one look or feel different—height, skin, hair, weight—these are the years when people are the most sensitive about how they differ from their classmates.

Some people have told me, "Being a tall girl is much worse than being short" or, "What girls go through is nothing compared to the agony of short boys!" And I've known very tall boys who have had their painful moments too.

In my research for this book I visited Glen Hills Middle School in Milwaukee, Wisconsin, where 271 students filled out a brief questionnaire about their height. They were particularly helpful in answering questions about how their height affects their feelings about themselves and how their height affects the way others treat them. Some of their comments are sprinkled throughout the book—often as picture captions—maybe you will identify with some of them.

CHAPTER
ONE

1

THE PROBLEMS
OF HEIGHT
. . . or,

"Why Can't I Look Like Everyone Else?"

Paul Powell is in trouble at school again.

"Why, Paul," the principal asks, "why do you always disrupt the class?"

Paul's stomach churns. The tall man towers over him. How can he explain? Sometimes he just likes to make the other kids laugh and pay attention to him. Today that big kid was teasing him again, calling him Small Paul.

"When the others tease you about being short, Paul, just ignore them. Don't worry. You'll grow. Try to behave yourself tomorrow."

Paul dashes out of the principal's office. "Don't worry, you'll grow"—oh, how he hates it when adults tell him that! He's twelve years old and in the seventh grade, but he knows that he looks like a fifth grader. He wants to grow *now*, not in the far distant future.

His friends have grown much taller, and they rub it in all the time, calling him Small Paul, Shortie, Shrimpo, even Toad.

3

"I don't fit in.... others think I'm immature."

Paul yanks open his locker. Next year they'll probably give me a top locker, he thinks in despair, and then I'll have to carry a stool to get at my books!

Everything reminds him of being the shortest in his class, not just the other kids, but also standing at the blackboard, lining up, or, worst of all, playing sports. He wants to play basketball and football like his friends, but he's afraid the coach won't let him if he doesn't grow soon. He's trying to work on his dribbling, because even a short kid can be good at that, but maybe he should quit.

Sometimes he feels that everyone treats him like a little kid, especially the girls. Next week there's a party, and he dreads it.

Paul slams his locker door. "I just wish I could be as big as everyone else!"

Bob Bonner reaches easily to the top shelf of his closet to grab his baseball mitt. He remembers that he couldn't do that last spring. Yesterday,

4

on his thirteenth birthday, his mother measured his height. He'd grown four inches in the past year.

He stares at himself in the full length mirror on the closet door. Inside he still feels like the same person, but he's shocked at what he sees— so tall and skinny, like a flagpole, long and narrow.

Bob's height is five feet seven inches, which is very tall for his age. Now he can look down at his mother. It takes getting used to, but Bob likes his tall height. It gives him a feeling of power. His parents and teachers treat him as if he were much older, and he likes that. But sometimes it's hard to act as old as everyone expects him to.

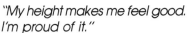
"My height makes me feel good. I'm proud of it."

The kids at school tease him a lot and call him Bird or Stork because of his long legs. They expect him to play great basketball, but Bob worries about being clumsy and uncoordinated, and

5

he'd rather play baseball anyway. He was just elected team captain. He can tell that the other guys wish they were as tall as he is, so it makes him proud. And he loves the way the girls pay attention to him.

Bob's cocker spaniel dashes into his room, and Bob dives for him, rolling over on the floor, the laughter and barking roaring through the house. Crash! They hit the bedside table and the lamp smashes to the floor.

"Oh, Bob, no!" His mother arrives breathless. "You're too big now to roughhouse like that!"

Bob can tell his mother isn't really mad, because she is pleased with his newly acquired height too. Of course it helps that the lamp didn't break! After straightening up the mess, Bob whistles on his way to the ball park, feeling good.

"Mom, did you know that Erma Bombeck is short?"

Pat Porter sits at the kitchen table reading her favorite newpaper column.

"What difference does it make, Pat? And why are you so obsessed lately with who's short?"

"Because if I'm going to be short, I want to find out how other people stand it. Listen to this. Erma Bombeck says when most people first see her they say, 'I thought you were taller!' So you know what she did? She walked out on stage and said to her audience, 'Gosh, I thought you'd all be taller!' "

Pat loves the comic twist because she's heard the standard comments about being short a zillion times. "Good things come in small packages" and "How's the weather down there?" have

"Since I'm small, I've been called wimp and a sissy."

become very boring. It never gets easier to know how to respond.

Being short didn't used to bother her. In fact, she liked being considered small and cute. Teachers always liked her and paid attention to her. Her parents didn't expect her to have as many responsibilities at home as her taller brother and sister. Since third grade the nickname "Peewee" meant that she was someone special. Everyone noticed her.

But now Pat is in seventh grade. At 4'5" she's the shortest in her class. She wants to be tall and slender, sophisticated and mature. She wants to wear all the new styles, but she still wears children's sizes. She hates being patted on the head. She feels that people look at her as if she were a brainless doll that's fun to play with, but not someone to take seriously. She wants to feel respected, like her tall friends.

"Erma Bombeck also says she's always hated being short and that 'people feel a compulsion to hug you because you remind them of a stuffed

7

animal they had as a child.' I know just what she means. I bet all short people feel the same way!"

Lisa Langley is also in seventh grade, and she's 5'8" tall. She's also very mature physically and has started her periods. She wears baggy sweaters to hide her bustline and she slouches down when she walks with her much shorter friends.

"If you feel too tall, you feel awkward and as if everyone is looking up to you."

Lisa, or "Long Lisa" as the boys call her, knows that models are tall and that many successful, beautiful women are tall. In fact, her height is the same as the average height for Miss America. She realizes that someday she'll like her height, but she wishes she hadn't grown tall so soon. It's embarrassing. She wants to look like her friends, not older. It makes her feel very confused. She likes being looked up to as a leader, but it's hard to act older all the time.

Her most embarrassing moment occurred last week when she and her mother were shopping. They were at the shoe store and she was agonizing over the huge boats she was trying on her feet, and who should walk in but a whole gang of her classmates. They couldn't believe she wears a size-ten shoe!

Some of the girls are catching up to her a little, and she loves playing on the new volleyball team, so maybe things will be better next year in eighth grade. When her friends talk about boys she says she doesn't care about them. It's not really true, but all the boys her age are so small compared to her, that she just ignores them. It doesn't seem fair to Lisa that girls have to grow up first!

Paul, Bob, Pat, and Lisa are reminded constantly that they look different from most of their friends. This difference causes situations and feelings that they can learn to understand and control.

Today there is a strong belief that "bigger is better. " Studies on height prejudice show that:

- Taller people often get better jobs and higher pay.
- Taller politicians are usually elected over shorter opponents. (Since 1900 only two presidents shorter than their opponents have been elected, Calvin Coolidge and Jimmy Carter. The shortest president was James Madison, 5'4".)

"I think my height makes me feel more confident."

- People with higher status seem to appear taller than colleagues of the same height. For example, a professor appears taller than a teacher's assistant.
- Throughout history the upper classes in society have been taller than the lower classes.
- There is a "halo effect" around talls because others react to them as being more intelligent, good-looking, likeable, convincing, capable.

Short people often feel "shortchanged," even "short-circuited," and, of course, "looked down on" for "shortcomings" (even everyday language reveals a prejudice against short people).

Short youngsters like Pat and Paul carry a double burden of not only overcoming the general prejudice, but also working harder to prove their increasing maturity. Growing up means growing taller. Staying little means staying a child. A lot of the belief in equating tallness with adulthood has to do with eye level. As young children we "look up to" our parents because they

10

"I feel weird next to people who are taller than me."

are so much taller. This physical act of looking up to those in authority becomes so embedded in our thinking that it's easy to assume that anyone we look up to is in a position of authority over us. That's why the phrase "look up to" also means "respect" and "admire."

Most young people today want to grow taller than average height. Of the middle-school students who answered a questionnaire, 83 percent of the boys want to be over 5'9", and 56 percent want to be at least 6'2". Of the girls, 83 percent want to be over 5'4", and 41 percent want to be at least 5'8".

But tall preteens and teenagers have problems too. They are thrust into leadership positions before they are ready for them, and they often wish they weren't so conspicuous.

If you think of yourself as tall or short, these questions might help you recognize your own behavior and see how it relates to your height. Sometimes awareness of potential problems can help eliminate them.

11

Dilemma of the Smalls

- If you want to be noticed, do you
    - . . . feel the need to talk a lot—and talk loudly?
    - . . . interrupt other people's conversation?
    - . . . enjoy it when a crowd is paying attention to you?
    - . . . act like a comedian, tell jokes, do imitations?
    - . . . cause trouble when you know you shouldn't?
- Do you feel inferior and
    - . . . get depressed easily?
    - . . . act as a younger child?
    - . . . feel frustrated and lonely?
    - . . . give up leadership to taller classmates?

Power of the Talls

- Do you feel pressured to be the decision maker for your group or to assume leadership positions such as class president, team captain?

- Do you strive to live up to others' expectations of you to act more maturely than your age? Is it difficult to act playful, childish?
- Do you find it sometimes difficult to convince others of your true age? Kareem Abdul-Jabbar, the 7'2" basketball player, was so tall as a child, he had to carry his birth certificate to prove his age for children's rates.
- Do you feel that you must restrain yourself, be careful not to hurt people with your bigger body?
- Do you feel afraid sometimes of acting clumsy or stupid the way comedians joke about tall people? A lot of Carol Burnett's humor stems from her uncomfortable feelings of being tall and clumsy as a preteen.

Accepting your height and learning how to use it to your advantage begins with understanding. The first step is to think about your height and how it got that way, and to learn about growth patterns. Here's what Pat and Paul, Bob and Lisa have discovered about their growth patterns.

Lisa is worried she'll keep growing into a giant. She is relieved to discover that her first menstrual period signalled the end of her most rapid growth. Now her growth rate is slowing down and will probably stop before she starts high school. Best of all, her feet have stopped growing!

"The Bird" doesn't care how tall he grows so long as his body fills out and he doesn't look like a beanpole. As he learns more about adolescent growth, he feels reassured that his legs won't get any longer and his shoulders will continue to grow much wider.

13

Small Paul thinks all his problems would be solved if only he didn't look so young. He learns from his doctor that he has inherited a late-growing pattern. The good news is he will grow a lot and may even end up taller than average because he has his whole adolescent growth phase ahead of him. The bad news is that he has to endure being short now when so many of his friends are growing taller and maturing rapidly.

"Sometimes I feel I'll get lost in a crowd."

Pat realizes that she comes from a short family and will probably not grow very tall. She'd better forget about being a model or a dancer. As she explores her growth pattern and stage of development, she learns she'll be lucky to hit five feet. Once she accepts that fact, she's happy to concentrate on taking advantage of the many pluses of being short.

CHAPTER TWO

PLOTTING YOUR GROWTH

. . . or,

"How Tall Will I Be?"

The most valuable tool in understanding your growth pattern is the growth chart. By marking your height at different ages you can discover:
- how your height compares to that of other American young people your age
- at what rate you are growing
- if your growth pattern is normal
- a rough guess at how tall you will grow

Height Comparisons

To compare your height to others in your age group, you need an accurate measurement. On page 18 are some tips on how to measure your height:

The body is taller in the morning. During a full night's sleep, the space between the bones spreads out, especially between the backbones. Adults can measure as much as one-half to a full inch taller when first rising. Then the tug of

Stand Tall!

chin even with
the floor

Use a wall
that's at a
right angle
to the floor

head, shoulders,
rear end, and
back of knees
pressed against
the wall

heel pressed
against the
right angle

bare feet

gravity during the day pulls the bones down and shrinks the spaces between. By evening the weight of the day has literally worn you down!

As you discover where your height is on the chart, note the wide range of normal sizes for your age. Older children and teenagers have a wider spread between tallest and shortest growth lines than younger children. We all start out at about twenty inches at birth, but adult normal height varies by ten inches between tallest and shortest.

18

GIRLS

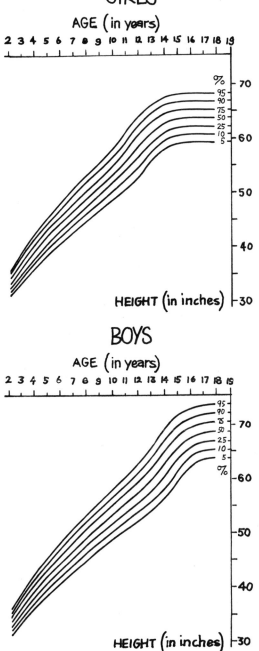

AGE (in years)

2 3 4 5 6 7 8 9 10 11 12 13 14 15 16 17 18 19

%
95
90
75
50
25
10
5

- 70
- 60
- 50
- 40
- 30

HEIGHT (in inches)

BOYS

AGE (in years)

2 3 4 5 6 7 8 9 10 11 12 13 14 15 16 17 18 19

95
90
75
50
25
10
5
%

- 70
- 60
- 50
- 40
- 30

HEIGHT (in inches)

The lines on these charts represent growth in height of the American population from age 2 to 19. The numbers on the seven lines, 5, 10, 25, 50, 75, 90 and 95, indicate the percentage of people who are shorter than that height line. For example, the 57" height of an 11-year-old boy is on the 75th-percentile line, which means that 75 percent of 11-year-old boys are shorter than he is, and therefore 25 percent are taller.

The middle line traces average height, with 50 percent of people taller and 50 percent shorter. Average adult height for women in the U.S. is a little under 5'5", and average height for men is just over 5'9". (Based on data from J.M. Tanner and P.S.W. Davis, Journal of Pediatrics, 1985: 107)

19

Growth Rate

The upward curve of the growth lines on the charts indicates how fast the height increases. The general shape of the curves shows fast growth during babyhood, slower growth during childhood, a fast spurt during adolescence, and a sharp slowdown into adulthood.

A general rule is that during the first year, a baby grows half of its birth length (birth length = 20 inches ÷ 2 = 10 inches), and during the second year, a child grows half of its first year growth (10 inches ÷ 2 = 5 inches).

From age two until adolescence, average yearly growth is $2\frac{1}{2}$ inches. Slow growers grow about two inches a year, while fast growers grow closer to three inches a year.

To trace your growth, you need a list of your height measurements at different ages. If you can get these from your doctor or parents, you can plot your own growth curve and see if you have been a slow or fast grower.

What's Normal?

A growth chart may reveal two clues indicating an abnormal growth pattern. One is a line that is traced above or below the top or bottom lines on the chart, indicating height that is within the tallest 5 percent or the shortest 5 percent of the population. Very tall or very short height may be a symptom of a problem needing medical treatment.

If your growth line falls above or below the chart lines, however, it doesn't necessarily mean there's something wrong with you. For example, my adult height of fifty-seven inches is far below

20

"I wish I was taller or shorter and not so average."

the 5 percent line on the girls' chart. Since my birth at eighteen inches, I've been much shorter than the bottom line, but there's nothing wrong with me. I simply come from a family of short people.

The second clue is a line that does not parallel the smooth curves of the standard growth charts. Healthy, normal growth follows a steady pace each year, although many children grow a little faster in the spring and summer than during the fall and winter. If you have been growing three inches a year and suddenly drop to two inches a year, an illness may be the cause. When a child grows less than two inches a year, a doctor will usually run tests to determine the reason. A growth line that looks more like jagged mountains than a smooth hill often indicates illness or a problem.

How Tall Will I Grow?

There is an "old wives' tale" that doubling the height at age two will predict the person's adult height. This prediction is often true, especially if the age is changed to twenty months for a girl and twenty-seven months for a boy.

To guess your adult height, find the line on the chart that matches your growth line and see where it ends at age nineteen.

These predictions are, of course, approximate, and doctors suggest allowing at least a two-inch margin of error either way. Your height will depend on many factors including the height of your parents and the growth potential you've inherited from them. Life-style factors, such as food and exercise, are also important.

Plotting your growth curve will help you see the whole pattern of your growth, both past and future. It will help you set realistic expectations about your height.

CHAPTER THREE

MYSTERY OF GROWING TALLER

. . . or,

"Did My Pants Shrink?"

Tammy yells down the stairs, "Mom, I can't find my favorite jeans!"

"Look in the dryer," her mother says.

Tammy runs down to the basement. If she doesn't hurry, she'll miss the school bus. She yanks the jeans out of the dryer and jams her legs through the holes. They feel soft and snug and familiar. She flies into the kitchen for a quick bowl of cereal.

"Tammy!" Her mother gasps and then laughs. "Either that dryer has really shrunk up those jeans, or you've grown!"

"Oh, no, that horrible dryer!" Tammy runs to the full-length mirror in the front hall. Her heart sinks when she sees the hem of the pants far above her shoes.

"It's not the dryer, Tammy. I've noticed them inching up on you. You'd be even madder if you didn't grow."

"Now what'll I wear?" Tammy is disgusted. It

25

"I love horses and always wanted to be a jockey, but I'm too tall. I really wanted to be short."

doesn't help that her mother is smiling as though she knows some secret.

The body usually grows so gradually during childhood that you don't notice it. When you suddenly realize, like Tammy, that your clothes are too small, you're inclined to blame it on the dryer. It's easier to understand clothes shrinking than the body growing—especially since you feel the same inside and you haven't noticed that you look different. But suddenly you realize that your body is growing—all the time, growing, growing.

Genetic Code: Your Biological Blueprint

You inherit from your parents the basic chemical units that direct the development of all your body cells. These chemical units are called *genes*.

The chemical makeup of genes is called "deoxyribonucleic acid," abbreviated DNA. DNA is the basic chemical unit of life, and therefore of growth. Everyone's DNA is made up of the same components, or building blocks, but they are arranged in a unique sequence in each person, called the *genetic code*.

One scientist estimated that the number of different ways the components of DNA can be arranged is 256 followed by 2.4 billion zeros. That's why there's a good chance no one else in the world can look exactly like you. Only identical twins have the same genetic codes.

Within the nucleus of living cells, enormously long strands of DNA intertwine. One scientist estimated that if all the DNA in the cells of a human body was untwisted and joined end to end, it would reach from the earth to the sun and back four hundred times. But in its natural state this same quantity of DNA is so tightly coiled that it would fit into a box the size of an ice cube.

The genes your mother has, which she inherited from *her* parents, directed her growth and helped determine her height. The same for your father. Now the combination in you of your parents' genes is directing your growth. That's why you will probably be short if your parents are short, or tall if they're tall. The pygmy tribes of Africa produce offspring with an average adult male height of 4½ feet. The world's tallest people also live in Africa—the Watusis. Their average adult male height is over 6 feet.

Bones: The Lengthening Structure

What actually creates height? The skeleton. Growing taller means growing longer bones, mainly in the legs and spine. Bones give your body rigidity so it won't collapse. All your mus-

Here's a guide for predicting your height
- *Measure your mother and father.*
- *If you're a girl, subtract 5" from your father's height. If you're a boy, add 5" to your mother's height. This adjustment accounts for the average height difference between men and women.*
- *Add the adjusted heights of your parents and divide by 2.*
- *To that number:*
    - *add 3¼" to determine the upper limit of your predicted height.*
    - *subtract 3¼" to determine the lower limit of your predicted height.*

Your final height has a 95 percent chance of falling within those two limits.

cles and flesh would flop in a heap without bones to hold them up!

To grow in length, a leg bone (and arm bone) adds cells to each end at the area called the growth plate. Growth plates are made up of cartilage cells, not hard bone cells. The very end of the

Simplified sketch of a growing leg bone.

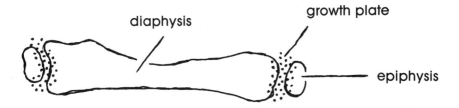

diaphysis

growth plate

epiphysis

bone is a knobby, hard part called the *epiphysis* (pronounced ee/PIF/ee/sis, from the Greek, meaning "to grow upon"). The growth plate lies in between the epiphysis and the long shaft part of the bone, called the *diaphysis* (di/AF/ee/sis, from the Greek, meaning "to grow between"). By adding bone cells to the shaft, the growth plate moves outward, pushing the knobby end in front of it.

Your legs grow longer mainly at the growth plates at the knees and at the ankles. There is little growth activity at the hip. In contrast, your arms grow mainly at the shoulders and wrists.

"I always try to feel as big as everyone else, and I have good friends even though I'm small."

Your spine grows longer at the growth plates in the vertebrae, the thirty-three bones of the spine. These small bones grow both upward and downward in equal amounts.

The skull and facial bones do not have growth plates. Their increase in size is caused by new layers of cells deposited on the outside of existing bones.

Of course while the bones are growing, all the muscles and tissues around them are growing too, but the lengthening bones provide the structural support and determine the height.

Many dwarfs are short because they have bone diseases which prevent the bones from growing normally. Billy Barty, the famous dwarf actor, is an example, as is Herve Villechaize, the actor who plays Tattoo on "Fantasy Island." Usually the dwarfs you see in the circus are short because of bone problems. In these disorders the legs and arms are shorter than normal in proportion to the trunk and head. These disorders occur when something goes wrong with the genetic code for bone growth, and, so far, doctors have been unable to find cause or cure.

Hormones: The Builders

Hormones, the body's builders, act like the brains of the operation. Nothing gets built without their direction. In fact, the word "hormone" means "to urge on."

Hormones are very tiny chemical agents that travel from one part of the body to another through the bloodstream. Glands that manufacture hormones are called *endocrine glands* (EN/do/krin is from the Greek, meaning "to sepa-

Many hormones from the pituitary gland influence growth

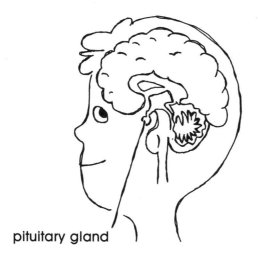

pituitary gland

rate"). The part of the body or cells that the hormones signal are called *target cells*. The target cells are separated from the endocrine glands, so the bloodstream is a handy transportation method, just like elevators. The whole system is called the *endocrine system* (which is why doctors who specialize in hormones are call *endocrinologists* - en/do/krin/OL/o/gists).

One of the most important endocrine glands, nicknamed "the master gland", is a little pea-size bag of cells nestled in the center of your head, straight back from the bridge of your nose. This structure is called the *pituitary gland* (pi/TOO/i/tar/y). It produces at least five different hormones that influence the body's growth. One is *human growth hormone,* often referred to as HGH, or simply growth hormone.

Human growth hormone signals the bones to grow. Without adequate production of this val-

"I pretend I'm 7' 7" and the greatest basketball player in the world."

uable builder, a child rarely grows taller than four feet, but will be normally proportioned.

Although he lived over a hundred years ago, circus performer Tom Thumb is still the most famous example of a man who grew up short because he lacked growth hormone. He was 3'4", or forty inches. He married Lavinia Bump, who was thirty-two inches. They were very popular with the public. The newlyweds were invited to the White House by tall President Lincoln, who remarked: "God likes to do funny things; here you have the long and the short of it."

The lack of HGH has caused the shortest heights on record. The *Guinness Book of World Records* lists the shortest adult human as Pauline Masters, a Dutch girl who was twelve inches long at birth in 1876. When she died at age nineteen, "Princess Pauline" measured 23.2 inches short. She never weighed more than nine pounds.

And what makes giants? One cause can be too much growth hormone. Just as something can go wrong with the pituitary gland so it doesn't produce any HGH, so can it produce far too much, causing the bones to grow in enormous excess. The tallest height recorded in *Guinness* is 8'11.1". This giant was Robert Wadlow. His legs were so long he didn't have any feeling below his ankles. He died in 1940 at age twenty-two of infection resulting from the rubbing of his ankle by an iron brace worn to help support his weight of almost five hundred pounds.

In normal growth, the pituitary shoots out bursts of HGH, particularly during deep sleep and exercise. Full grown adults often are surprised to learn that HGH is produced all their lives and it helps metabolize food. HGH is an extremely important messenger for many body activities.

Another hormone from the pituitary goes to the thyroid gland in the neck. Without enough thyroid hormone, most cells function too slowly to allow normal growth. Other pituitary hormones are concerned with stimulating the production of sex hormones, which influence growth during sexual maturation and final growth.

That's a lot of hormones—and we haven't even mentioned them all! The body produces at least a dozen hormones that affect the growth process. The important thing to understand is that your body needs a lot of workers to grow right, and if one of them is lazy, the whole body suffers.

Genetic code, bones, hormones—these are part of your biological inheritance as a human being. You don't have much control over them. But you do have some control over other factors that affect your growth—environmental factors. The most important ones are health, food, exercise, sleep, and love.

Tammy's mother smiles at her daughter's predicament with the short jeans because she's happy the mystery of growth is operating just the way it's supposed to. All she needs to do about it is buy Tammy new jeans. And all Tammy needs to do is decide what to wear today—and she'd better hurry or she'll miss the school bus!

CHAPTER
FOUR

4

PRETEEN AND TEENAGE GROWTH
. . . or,

"When Will It Happen to Me?"

When I was in seventh grade, I was a full head shorter than everyone else in my class, so I looked very young, especially from the back. From a front view it was obvious that I was maturely developed. How embarrassing! Most of the other girls in my class looked almost flat, and they were lots taller than I was.

In the locker room I became an expert at changing in and out of my gymsuit without exposing my body. I was ashamed of it. I looked very different from all my friends, mainly because of my short height.

Looking different can be painful. The irony is that looking different usually happens during the preteen and teenage years, when looking the same is the most important. Both words "adolescence" and "puberty" refer to this stage of growth, when physical, emotional, and mental changes pave the way for the child to grow into an adult.

37

Right before puberty begins, growth in height lags. In many boys it slows almost to a complete halt. Then comes the final burst, the shooting up to maturity. This last growth spurt varies widely between boys and girls in timing (when it begins) and in vigor (how long it lasts and how much growth occurs). It is not nearly as predictable as childhood growth, but here are some general observations:

- The physical changes of adolescence usually take about four to five years, although they can take anywhere from 1½ to 6 years.
- On average, girls have their growth spurt about two years before boys.

"Sometimes I feel alienated from my friends. I intimidate some of them."

- Boys grow more during puberty than girls.
- Growth in height speeds up for about three years, with the peak rate occurring in the second year of the spurt. In boys the average peak rate of growth is 3½ inches between ages

thirteen and fourteen. In girls the average peak rate of growth is 3¼ inches between ages eleven and twelve. After these peaks, growth in height tapers off.

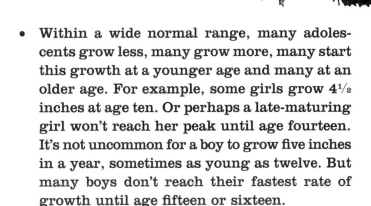

"They don't like me because I'm too big."

- Within a wide normal range, many adolescents grow less, many grow more, many start this growth at a younger age and many at an older age. For example, some girls grow 4½ inches at age ten. Or perhaps a late-maturing girl won't reach her peak until age fourteen. It's not uncommon for a boy to grow five inches in a year, sometimes as young as twelve. But many boys don't reach their fastest rate of growth until age fifteen or sixteen.

Tom is a typical boy whose adolescent changes follow the average pattern. At age twelve Tom is almost five feet tall. At the onset of puberty the increased flow of male sex hormones influence his growth. These hormones, called androgens (AN/dro/gen—*andro* is Greek for "man"), cause a boy to turn into a man sexually. The major male sex hormone is testosterone (tes/TOS/ter/one) and is produced by the male sex glands, the

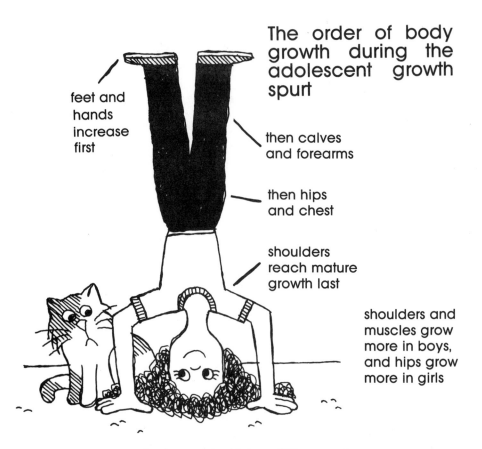

The order of body growth during the adolescent growth spurt

feet and hands increase first

then calves and forearms

then hips and chest

shoulders reach mature growth last

shoulders and muscles grow more in boys, and hips grow more in girls

testes or testicles. Other androgens are manufactured in the adrenal glands, located on top of the kidneys.

The slow trickle of sex hormones grows to a flood, triggering many dramatic changes. First his genital organs (testes and penis) begin to enlarge and mature. Then his hands and feet seem much too large for the rest of him. Pubic hair, facial hair, and an increasing feeling of confidence and strength add slowly to changes that make him look different, act different, and feel different. He can't trust his voice to stay at one pitch, but he is glad to hear the new, lower

40

sounds. No one recognizes his voice when he answers the phone, which is both embarrassing and fun.

Tom is growing at the fastest rate since he was a toddler of two. In his fourteenth year, at the peak of his adolescent growth spurt, he grows almost four inches. By the time he is sixteen, his trunk is in proportion to his long legs and arms, and he is fully mature sexually. By age eighteen his chest and shoulders are a robust size, and his height levels off at almost 5'10".

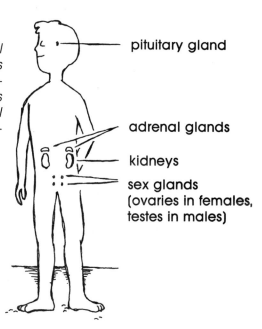

Puberty begins with a hormonal "quadruple play." Hormones from the brain stimulate the pituitary gland to send hormones to the sex glands and adrenal glands, which send out sex hormones to the whole body.

pituitary gland

adrenal glands

kidneys

sex glands
(ovaries in females,
testes in males)

Authorities say most modern males have reached 99.8 percent of their adult height by age eighteen or nineteen.

What about girls? If male sex hormones cause the male growth spurt, do female sex hormones cause the female growth spurt?

The answer is NO!

The same *male* androgens help cause the growth spurt in females too! The adrenal glands in both sexes produce androgens, and during puberty this production is radically increased—not enough in girls to cause beard growth, but enough to promote a surge of bone growth. The female sex glands, the ovaries, produce female sex hormones which also contribute to the general growth spurt in early puberty.

"Sometimes being tall makes me feel graceful, mature, more sophisticated. But short people are so cute! Short girls seem to get all the attention, especially from the boys."

Sally is a typical girl whose growth follows the average adolescent pattern. She matures earlier than Tom. Her growth begins to speed up when she is ten and a half. Other body changes happen rapidly—breast development, pubic and underarm hair, genital development, rounded hips. When she is thirteen she has her first menstrual period (menarche, pronounced men/AR/kee, from the Greek work *arche* meaning beginning). By fourteen, Sally's height is tapering to a halt at 5′5″. At age fourteen Tom finally catches up to Sally and zooms taller in the next four years.

Tom grows taller than Sally because he had extra years for more childhood growth before his pubertal growth spurt began, and because he has more male sex hormones to boost the vigor of the growth spurt.

Growth in height stops because the cartilage cells in the bones' growth plates stop responding to growth hormone (HGH). This is a gradual process, and as growth slows down, the plates get thinner and thinner. Finally the entire bone fuses together and the growth plates are eliminated. No further growth in length is possible.

"Sometimes some of my friends are scared of me when I get mad or annoyed."

This closing process is caused in part by the sex hormones, both testosterone and the female hormone estrogen. Yes—the same hormones that cause growth to speed up also cause it to stop! How can that be? Scientists aren't sure. They think it may be connected to the supply of hormones; smaller amounts early in puberty promote increased growth, but the larger doses in

GIRLS

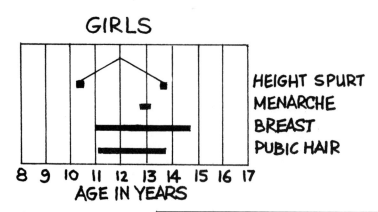

HEIGHT SPURT
MENARCHE
BREAST
PUBIC HAIR

8 9 10 11 12 13 14 15 16 17
AGE IN YEARS

Sequence of Events of Puberty.

These charts show the sequence of four pubertal changes in boys and girls at average ages. The majority of boys start these changes between the ages of 9½ and 13½. The majority of girls start these changes between the ages of 8 and 13. Although the speed of development can be slower or faster than shown, the sequence of when these changes occur is almost always the same.

These charts show when your height spurt will most likely occur. If you are a girl and you've had your first period, your height peak has probably passed, and you are almost finished growing. If you are a boy who is just beginning to notice some sexual changes, your height spurt has barely begun.

BOYS

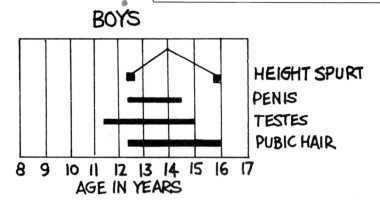

HEIGHT SPURT
PENIS
TESTES
PUBIC HAIR

8 9 10 11 12 13 14 15 16 17
AGE IN YEARS

late puberty and early adulthood signal the end of bone growth. One study has shown that in boys between ages ten and seventeen, the amount of testosterone multiplied twentyfold.

Because you'll reach 98 percent of your height by the end of adolescence, we consider that growth stops there. But to be exact, your vertebrae in the spinal column will grow a tiny bit more until about age thirty. The size of your head will increase slightly all your life. So will the width of the bones in your legs and hands. From about age thirty to forty-five, height stays about the same. Then you'll start to shrink! With age, the bones tend to thin and press together, causing some reduction in height.

Dr. James Tanner, a world famous British growth expert, has studied adolescent growth for years. His discoveries concerning the sequence of changes that all adolescent boys and girls encounter can help you understand your own growth.

Chuck at age sixteen is 5'9" and hopes he'll grow several more inches. But Chuck is maturely developed, so he has probably reached the extent of his growth spurt. Dr. Tanner notes that another indicator of the late stage of puberty is full beard growth and voice change. And the fact that Chuck shaves every day also tells them that his growth is generally finished.

Heather is in seventh grade and expects to be at least 5'3" like her mother. But she started her periods last year and now her height is 4'10". Five more inches is probably an impossibility. But Susan, who's 5'10", is thrilled to know that her periods signal the tapering off of her growth.

Bobby, like many short boys, is relieved to know

that he is just a "late bloomer" like his dad and that nothing's wrong with him. A small boy, Dr. Tanner notes, "whose genitalia are just beginning to develop, can be unequivocally reassured that an acceleration in height is soon to take place."

By noticing these changes in your body, you can predict the path your growth will follow. If your parents can remember the timing and speed of their trip through puberty, that will help you judge your own. The genetic code you've inherited from them directs the pace of your growth, especially during adolescence.

"I'm easy to pick on because I'm short."

CHAPTER
FIVE

5

ENVIRONMENTAL FACTORS

. . . or,

"Do I Have to Eat That?"

"I want to lose a lot of weight fast!"

Eleven-year-old Susie looks with despair at the fitting-room mirror. The new pants sag in a puddle on the floor, miles too long. The top droops to her knees.

"A size that's big enough to fit around my fat body is long enough to fit a giant," she moans to her mother. "I'm just too short and fat!"

Susie thinks that all clothes are designed for the tall and slender. She hates the way she looks. She hates her mother for saying she'll look fine with everything shortened. Most of all, she hates herself.

Since she can't stretch out her body to fit the pants, she thinks her only option is to lose weight so she can fit into a smaller size.

A recent study by researchers in California reports that four-fifths of girls in the fourth grade are dieting. By junior or senior high, almost every girl thinks about losing weight. But studies also

show that chronic dieting often causes poor eating patterns, and one result of major under-nutrition in preteens and teenagers can be stunted growth.

Unless Susie is excessively heavy, if she keeps her weight steady without gaining, her continued growth in height will cause her to become both taller and slimmer. Susie and anyone who wants to lose weight should talk with a nutritionist first.

Of course food is essential for all growth and good health. "You are what you eat" is basically true. We only need to look at photos of starving children in Africa to see what famine can do. These children are not growing at all. Even with plenty of calories, if enough protein isn't digested, cells can't grow in size. Vitamins and minerals are also needed to reach height potential.

Major Vitamins and Minerals Needed for Healthy Bone Growth	
Nutrient	**Source**
Vitamins:	
A	liver, orange vege-tables, & fruits
C	fruits, leafy green vegetables
D	milk, cheese, fish oils
Minerals:	
Calcium	milk, cheese
Phosphorus	milk, cheese
Zinc	animal products
Potassium	in many foods, esp. green leafy vegetables
Iron	liver, red meat, turkey, dried fruit, beans, egg yolk.

Improved nutrition and better medical care have produced dramatic results. During the last hundred years the average adult height has grown one centimeter (or about one-third of an inch) every ten years, an increase of over three inches. Children's average heights have grown even more because they are reaching maturity more rapidly. In the early 1900s most men did not stop growing until age twenty-five or twenty-six, but now that age has dropped to about eighteen. Earlier maturation also means that girls start their periods at a younger age. Now the average age is thirteen, but a hundred years ago it was sixteen. One of the major causes of this trend is an increased supply of calories and protein.

Does this mean average height will continue to go up and up until humans are giants? Or that people will mature earlier and earlier until childhood will flash by in a year or two? No. Scientists think that in the U.S. we've nearly reached the limits of our genetic potential. They also agree that the wide range of heights has been unaffected over the years. No matter what the average height, there will always be short people and tall people.

The influence of food on growth is called an environmental or external factor. Other important environmental factors that affect your height are illness, sleep, exercise, and good old-fashioned TLC (you know, tender loving care!).

ILLNESS

The body must be healthy and free of serious illness to grow properly. A good example is Scott Hamilton, the Olympic gold-medal figure skater whose height was stunted in childhood because of disease. Another example is the actor Gary Coleman, who is very short because of kidney problems.

EXERCISE

Both bones and muscles respond to the stress of exercise by growing stronger. When the bones are not exercised, they become soft and weak. When muscles are not exercised they wither and shrink.

Boys' muscle growth (in both number and size of muscle cells) far exceeds girls'. Although the

sexes start about even at birth, by three weeks
of age boys already have more muscle cells than
girls. By age ten, a girl will have about five times
as many muscle cells as when she was born, and
little further increase occurs. But a boy's muscle
cells continue to multiply until, at age eighteen,
he has at least fourteen times as many as he had
at birth. And they may continue to enlarge for
another five years.

Exercise also improves coordination, balance,
and agility. During the rapid and uneven growth
of adolescence, these qualities help combat awk-
wardness, clumsiness, poor posture, and the
general feeling of strangeness with one's own
body.

SLEEP

Deep sleep is a stimulus to the output of growth
hormone. That doesn't mean that if you sleep
more you'll grow taller. But studies show that
children whose sleep is too light and too brief
grow less than during times of peaceful, deep

rest. The rapid adolescent growth spurt can cause extra fatigue.

ATTENTION

You need a loving home in which to grow. Children who are severely deprived of love and attention may not grow even if they are given plenty to eat. The cause is usually due to anxiety and emotional upset. Sometimes the emotional trauma of severe starvation for love will shut down the production of growth hormone.

Scientists are proving the important influence of our emotional state on our bodily functions, including growth. Anxiety interferes with digestion, which can prevent nutrients from reaching the growing cells. Anxiety also interferes with sleep.

All of these environmental factors play big roles in determining your height. So if you want to find out "How tall will I be?", you should also ask, "How healthy am I? Am I eating right? Do I get enough exercise? Do I get peaceful, deep sleep? Do I feel loved and happy?"

There's another question you should ask yourself, too. Am I deliberately putting anything into my body that will hurt my growth?

Tobacco   Alcohol   Marijuana   Cocaine

The chemicals that are absorbed into the system by the use of any of these drugs, plus many more, can be very harmful to the growth process.

A recent report from the U.S. Office on Smoking and Health indicates that youngsters may suffer *immediate* lung damage when they take up smoking, not merely run the risk of disease in the distant future. Healthy lungs are necessary for all growth processes of the body.

In addition to lung damage, studies on the smoking of marijuana show that this drug lowers the output of growth hormone and both male and female sex hormones.

Alcohol is a depressant and alters brain cells, slowing many body processes. The smaller the body, the quicker and deeper the effect. Alcohol is a dehydrator and washes away vitamin C, calcium, potassium, and magnesium—all necessary ingredients for proper bone growth.

Cocaine also alters brain chemistry, sometimes permanently, and brain cells that are damaged can never be replaced.

Many young people experiment with these and other drugs. One of many damaging effects can be stunted growth.

CHAPTER
SIX

6

SEEING
A DOCTOR
. . . or,
"Isn't There a Hormone I Can Take?"

One of the most common reasons adolescents see doctors is because they don't like their body size—usually because they're short and want to grow taller.

Since many childhood diseases now are prevented by vaccines or helped with modern drugs, doctors have more time to study the growth process and try to find cures for some of the things that go wrong with growth. The Human Growth Foundation in Bethesda, Maryland, reports that there are at least a half million children with severe growth problems and over a hundred reasons why their growth patterns aren't normal.

Some clues that warn of possible problems and signal a need to discuss growth with a doctor are:
- still wearing last year's clothes or outgrowing clothes much faster than usual
- growing less than two inches or more than three inches in a year

"I feel like some kind of a wimp. People think they can walk all over me because I'm small."

- showing signs of early sexual development before age seven for girls and age nine for boys
- not showing any signs of sexual development by age thirteen for girls or age fifteen for boys

To evaluate a growth problem, the doctor will check height records and family history and do a complete physical examination. He may also order some laboratory tests such as urine and blood tests. Sometimes growth-hormone level is tested, often by taking blood samples during a series of exercises.

X-rays of bones of the wrist indicate "bone age." If you are ten years old and have a bone age of eight, it means your bones are in the growth stage of the average eight-year-old, so your bones are developing slowly. For short children, it's a very hopeful sign to have a delayed bone age, because it means that there is more growth potential in their bones than their true age would indicate.

The largest group of short boys who see doctors about their growth are "late bloomers". The doctors' long name for this pattern is "constitutional growth delay with delayed adolescence." There is nothing physically wrong with the person, but the genes dictate a delay in the onset of puberty. Many more boys than girls are affected. They are small for their age during

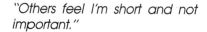
"Others feel I'm short and not important."

childhood and start adolescence two to four years later than their friends. A fourteen-year-old boy with severe growth delay may look like a nine- or ten-year-old. The emotional anguish of this growth pattern can be painful, with effects lasting long after normal height and development have been reached. A doctor's advice on coping with this problem can be helpful.

Some growth problems are caused by a faulty genetic structure. One example is Turner's Syndrome which affects girls and causes immature sexual development and short height. Adults measure 4'7" to 4'10".

HIYA!

"Around shorter people I want to slouch! In third grade I felt as though I stuck out like a sore thumb."

Another example is Marfan's Syndrome which causes very tall stature and weak connective tissues. Some authorities believe Abraham Lincoln (6'4") had Marfan's Syndrome. Basketball players are now tested for this problem because the weak tissue can cause major blood vessels to break during extreme pressure. The great woman volleyball player Flo Hyman (6'5") died during a game, and it was discovered on autopsy that she was a victim of Marfan's.

An exciting area of treatment in recent years has been the use of human growth hormone. HGH was first isolated and used for treatment in 1957. Since then, over ten thousand children who lack natural production of this hormone have reached

"If you're short, the big guys don't want to play with you, so they beat you up."

heights of over five feet with the help of growth-hormone injections. For many years the supply was limited because the only method of obtaining HGH was removing it from pituitary glands of people who had died. But then scientists discovered how to manufacture HGH through new techniques of genetic engineering. In 1985 the synthetic HGH was approved for doctors' use by the Federal Drug Administration. With the increased supply, scientists are testing its use on other causes of short height, such as Turner's Syndrome.

If you're not as tall as you'd like to be, don't assume that a shot of HGH will help you grow. When the body is producing growth hormone normally, short height is due to other factors. Adding unneeded growth hormone might shut off a person's natural production, or it might create an unhealthy abundance. Overproduction of growth hormone in adults produces a condition called "acromegaly," in which there is a grotesque enlargement of the bones of the hands, feet, and face. Too much growth hormone may also produce high blood pressure, diabetes, and heart disease.

"My height makes me work harder in sports."

When a committee of doctors who are experts in growth research recently studied the use of growth hormone in normal children, they concluded that the best advice is to follow the old saying, "If it ain't broke, don't fix it."

Other hormones are used effectively when the natural supply is low. Thyroid-hormone pills easily correct thyroid deficiency, which can slow growth. The addition of sex hormones can sometimes be very helpful. For example, girls with Turner's Syndrome lack ovaries, so they cannot produce their own estrogen. Hormone treatment helps them achieve sexual maturity.

Treatment with sex hormones has also been given to late-developing boys to speed up the start of adolescence, and to tall girls to help stop growth. Both of these treatments are controversial.

The addition of the male hormone testosterone helps small boys grow up, but it can cause problems too. One danger is that the speeded-up timing of puberty may also speed up the closing of the growth plates so that the boy may never reach as tall a height as he would normally.

Young girls whose predicted heights are at least six feet have been given estrogen to help force sexual maturation and slow down growth. But the unknown, long-term risks of this hormone treatment may not be worth the height reductions, which have averaged one-half to three inches.

The risks and benefits of hormone therapy must be assessed individually for every person.

If you are disturbed about your height, it's good to discuss your questions with your doctor. It's always the wisest course to make sure all

your biological systems are "go." Discuss your eating habits and exercise routine with the doctor also—perhaps there is something you can do yourself to help your body develop so that it will be more pleasing to you.

After you have examined the physical you, take a look at the psychological you. If you think your height is a handicap, perhaps the best treatment is to think about how to like yourself. And maybe you'll learn to like your height.

CHAPTER
SEVEN

LIKING
YOUR HEIGHT
. . . or,
"I Feel Good About Myself!"

Sandy Allen, the world's tallest woman at 7'7¼",
has said, "If I could choose to be 5'6" tomorrow,
I don't think that I would do it. I have accepted
myself, and I think I like myself fine just the
way I am." At the other extreme is movie star
Michael Dunn, who was 3'10". He said, "My life
has been just like everyone else's—finding out
what you can do, what you like to do, and doing
it."

If Sandy Allen and Michael Dunn could over-
come the disadvantages of their sizes, accept
themselves, and make a success of their lives, so
can you.

Accepting yourself is a result of feeling comfortable with yourself, and there are lots of things
you can do to help promote that feeling.

How Do You Fit?

Think about how you fit into your physical environment. At home, notice what you use every

"Sometimes I feel out of place, but most of the time I feel good about myself."

day. If you can't see well in the bathroom mirror, see about hanging another one that suits you. If everything in the kitchen that you like to use is beyond easy reach, talk to your mother about some rearranging—glasses don't have to be on a top shelf.

Often it's hard for short people to find a satisfactory place to do homework because they're overwhelmed by too-high desks and tables, and it's uncomfortable to sit for long with feet dangling. A drafting table with an adjustable stool may be better if you're short or tall. A comfortable chair and a lap board also work well.

Be both realistic and creative about altering your home environment to fit your size. It's difficult to change things at school, but there are always ways to get around the obstacles. All short students are fast at spotting chairs with rungs on which to hook their feet.

Often the last choice when things are hard to reach is to ask for help, but it may be the best choice. If you smile and ask in good humor, you will make a friend. People really like to help others. It makes them feel good.

To help boost your positive attitude, appreciate all the things that are easier for you because

you're either short or tall. There are lots of small places where being little is an advantage, such as on an airplane. And being tall is a great advantage in a crowd.

How Do You Look?

Make the most of your physical appearance. There is always pleasure in looking one's best. The rules to follow whether you are short or tall are:
- Dress to suit your age.
- Make sure your clothes fit properly.
- Don't wear extreme styles.

Dressing to suit your age will help enforce the impression of your true age even though your height may make you look younger or older.

If you are in a rapid-growth phase, keep your wardrobe limited but current with your size, even if it means buying new pants every two months.

It can be embarrassing to shop in a department that you don't feel is appropriate for your age. If you're short enough to need clothes from the children's department, grin and bear it for the sake of looking your best. Shop for the right fit when you're feeling very "up" and proud of yourself.

Finding the right style is often harder than finding the right fit. A scientist who studies how people feel about their bodies says that when we aren't sure of ourselves, we try to reinforce the image of our bodies by clothing them in vivid colors or extreme styles to attract attention. In this way clothing becomes sort of a security blanket to reassure ourselves of our physical boundaries.

If you are uncomfortable about looking separate from the pack because of your height, don't buy clothes that draw attention.

Tips for girls:
- If you think you look very small and young for your age, be careful about trying to change your image with too much makeup, too much jewelry, or a hairstyle that's for much older teenagers and not right for you.
- Create your appearance to suit your age, not older. If you are tall, you may be tempted to emphasize your older, more sophisticated image by dressing to that look—and most of the fashions, including makeup and jewelry, are easily available to help you. But remember, the older you look, the more will be expected of you.
- Have your best colors analyzed by a color con-

sultant. It's a good way to learn how to look better and feel positive about yourself.

While you're thinking about how you look, pay attention also to how you sound. The impression your voice makes on others is part of your personal appearance. If you're small and you're having trouble with being treated as though you were younger, make sure your voice sounds your true age and not childish or whiny. If you are having trouble making a good first impression, be sure your voice carries a friendly note and not an antagonistic or bullying one.

What Do You Do?

Spend your time on activities that are either suited to your size or don't depend upon size—activities that will help you feel good about yourself. The variety is almost endless. Here are some major categories for you to think about:

EDUCATION

Oh no, you say, not schoolwork! Well, yes! Learning *can* be fun and a great morale booster. Good grades are positive feedback. Reading for pleasure is not only educational but a great escape from the daily grind.

There are other interesting and rewarding projects available besides regular school work. How about creating something for a science fair? Or learning a foreign language? What about becoming proficient on a computer and learning about different software? The equipment may be available at your local library. And don't forget your spiritual education—church and synagogue classes and youth groups are easily available.

"People think I'm older and better at sports."

WANT TO PLAY ON OUR TEAM?

SURE... UH...WHAT IS THAT SPHERICAL OBJECT YOU ARE HOLDING?

SPORTS

Whatever your height, having a fit body will help you look good, plus feel good. Any exercise will help, but participating in sports can be the key to an achievement that will be very satisfying.

I can hear someone out there yelling, "Sports! I'm too small for sports!"

All sports require strength, but a tall body isn't automatically strong and a short body isn't necessarily weak. The National Athletic Health Institute compared the physical attributes of many top athletes from various sports—football, baseball, tennis, etc. Who scored the highest in the battery of conditioning tests? Bill Shoemaker, the winningest jockey of all time. According to the report, "Jockeys as a group have the best overall conditioning of all athletes. . . . Billy Shoemaker is in better physical shape than many of the Los Angeles Rams." "The Shoe" stands about 4'10" and can weigh in at 103 pounds, including his saddle.

Unfortunately, in some schools it's difficult for short boys to excel in sports because of the emphasis on the big three in which height has a definite advantage—football, basketball, and baseball. But many schools are now including soccer, track, tennis, volleyball, or swimming, and short kids have a better chance in these sports.

One handsome 5'2" high-school senior explained to me that he has specialized in diving because, "A short person looks like he's bouncing higher in the air off the board, and I have more room to do stunts before I enter the water."

There are several successful professional athletes who are short for their games, for example football player Mark Duper (Miami Dolphins) is 5'9", and basketball player Spud Webb (Atlanta Hawks) is only 5'7". So if you're 4'5" and you're dying to be a basketball player, don't let me discourage you! But it just might be worth your time to find out what other sports options are open to you.

Sports That Favor Talls and/or Bigs

Basketball
Football
Baseball
Discus and javelin throwing
High and broad jumping
Running races, especially hur-
    dles and sprints
Boxing, except lightweight
Wrestling, except lightweight
Rowing
Cycling, sprints
Swimming, sprints

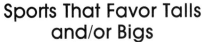

Sports For Smalls and Everyone

Soccer
Tennis
Hockey—ice and field
Skating—ice and roller
Pole vaulting
Swimming, esp. * long distance, racing, synchronized
* Diving
Skateboarding
* Weight lifting
Golf
* Skiing—snow and water
Squash
Racquetball
Handball
* Horseback riding, esp. racing, rodeo riding
Car racing
Bowling
* Gymnastics
Sledding
Fishing
Jogging
* Long-distance running
* Cycling, long distance
Boating
Archery
Fencing
Lacrosse
* Wrestling (weight divisions)
* Surfing
Volleyball
Karate

especially good for smalls

THE ARTS

Music . . . art . . . theater . . . dance. All four of these activities are wide open. Almost every community has opportunities for young people to develop interests in these areas. It's up to you to give it a try.

It sounds silly to say, "I can't play the violin—I'm too short," but sometimes it's easy to feel that way. The mind set of feeling inadequate can tempt you into the false belief that you're not capable of doing anything well. Be sure to free yourself of that temptation and assert yourself in a creative activity.

HOBBIES

This category includes *everything*—photography, carpentry, needlework, stamp collecting, model-ship building, cooking, tinkering with car engines, rebuilding grandfather clocks, and much more. What do *you* do? What would you like to do? Pick something that's fun, something that when you finish a project, you say to yourself, "Hey, I did it!" and that makes you feel good about yourself. Who knows? It may become a hobby you'll enjoy all your life.

The three main ways to develop a positive feeling about yourself, making yourself more comfortable in your environment, making the most of your appearance, and spending time on activities that you enjoy, are important. But the *most* important way is receiving positive feedback from the people you care about.

In fact, perhaps the most profound influence on how you feel about yourself is your ability to make friends and maintain relationships.

What to Do about Teasing

All very short or very tall people have experienced teasing.

"How's the weather up/down there?"

"You can stand up now!"

"Get out of the hole!"

Scientists say that teasing is an impulsive result of anxiety. In other words, your peers notice your height and feel uncomfortable because of being either shorter or taller than you. So their discomfort often makes their mouths work faster than their brains. And the teasing comments put you in a state of anxiety. So all this anxiety needs defusing before it explodes, and it's up to you to do it.

"I feel I don't fit. In basketball the tall people are picked."

Some actual teasing comments and responses:

"You are tall." "It runs in the family."

"How can you get the basketball up to the net?" "Just as well as you can."

"You're so short!" "Gosh, I guess I didn't notice that until you told me!"

"You're just too short." "It's normal, and I'll sprout up soon."

"How's the weather up there?" "It's raining."

"You're so short!" "I'd rather be short than a bean pole!"

"How's the weather?" "Just the same as it is down there!"

"Why are you so short?" "Because short people are more lovable."

"You're short!" "Thanks for telling me!"

"I feel so short around you!" "You're not that short!"

First, don't let yourself be too vulnerable. Relax. The teasing makes you angry, but it's part of life and you can handle it.

Second, have a reply ready so you don't have to think about it, and you can get past the moment without being dragged into a state of anger or embarrassment that will spoil your day. It doesn't really matter *what* you say. Something quick and simple, such as "Everyone has their problems" will do. It does matter *how* you say it—with a smile. The comedienne Phyllis Diller says, "A smile is a curve that sets everything straight."

Let your self-confidence and acceptance of your height radiate so that the person teasing you will be put at ease. Don't be aggressive about it. Just be direct and show good humor. Minimize the situation. Then move on to other conversation.

A sense of humor can solve awkward situations. Here's what Chicago Bears' William "Refrigerator" Perry says about his size (6'2", 308 pounds): "I've always thought that if you're different, it's up to you to make friends with the other guy. My sense of humor can carry me. I laugh along. I figure that God shapes everybody to a purpose."

Basketball player Manute Bol (7'7") has become experienced at fielding comments from the vocal American public since he left his homeland in Africa. When begged to stand up, he answers, "Can't. Leg broke." He answers the stares with, "I'm a good-looking guy." When asked, "What size shoes do you wear?" he smilingly answers, "You want to buy me a pair?" (He wears size 15½.)

On the questionnaire the students shared these nicknames.

HIYA, SHRIMPO!

HI, FROG LEGS!

BOYS

For Smalls
Short Stuff
Sparky
Little Leftover
Shortie
Shrimp
Squirt
Little Man
Runt
Peewee
Dip
Smurf
Wedge
Shrimpo
Toad

For Talls
Ape
Too Tall
The Vanilla Gorilla
Moose Man
Long Legs
Frog Legs

GIRLS

For Smalls	*For Talls*
Shortie	Too Tall
Sprout	Centipede
Shrimp	Grasshopper
Minnie Mouse	Toothpick
Little Bug	Skinny
Short Stuff	Mama Long Legs
Short Fry	Jolly Green Giant
French Fry	Tree
Chipmunk	

Let Your Height Be a Friend-Maker

If you're small, make use of the strength of being unthreatening to others. Small is the only universal size—everyone knows what it's like. Smaller people often fear taller people and feel intimidated, but no one fears someone smaller. As one researcher commented, "Midgets have always been more popular than giants."

Smallness, as one shortie noted, can be "like a surprise weapon. Nobody expects that much from you, so when you deliver, they're impressed."

Being short or tall can make friends for you because of the same reason you don't like your height: it makes you different. People notice you and remember you. You won't fade into the crowd. Because you are easily noticed, the first hurdle in making friends is jumped. Then comes the hard part: building the friendships.

The syndicated columnist, Ann Landers, gives this advice, "All people enjoy being around someone who is interesting and who makes them feel good. People enjoy the company of someone who is interested in *them*." Don't let your size become an obsession. Forget yourself and think about others, and your reward will be many friends.

Whether you are growing up small or tall, perhaps the best advice comes from a 5'1" eighth-grade boy: "Life goes on no matter what seems wrong to you. I try to roll with the punches and not let it get me down. I think people like me for what's inside." And a 5'8" eighth-grade girl: "Most often I really believe people look at me for what I am and not my height. Height doesn't interfere with friendship."

83

Index

Illness, 52

Landers, Ann, 83
Lincoln, Abraham
    and Marfan's syndrome, 62
    and Tom Thumb, 32

Marfan's syndrome, 62
Measuring height. *See* Height,
    how to measure
Menarche, 42, 44
Menstruation. *See* Menarche
Muscle growth, 52–53

Nicknames, 82. *See also* Teasing
Nutrition and diet, 49–52

Ovaries. *See* Sex glands

Perry, William, 81
Physical appearance, 71–73
Physical environment, 69–71
Pituitary gland, 31–33, 41
Prejudice against short people,
    9–11. *See also* Teasing
Presidents (U.S.), 9, 62
Puberty. *See* Adolescence
Pygmies, 27

Self-image
    during adolescence, 37, 59
    how to improve, 69–83
Sex glands, 40–42. *See also* Sex
    hormones
Sex hormones
    effect on bone growth, 39–43
    stimulation of, 33
    treatment with, 65
Sexual changes, 40, 42, 44. *See
    also* Adolescence
Sexual maturation. *See* Adoles-
    cence
Shoemaker, Bill, 75

Shortest adult human, 32
Shortest human group, 27
Sleep, 53–54
Smoking, 55. *See also* Drugs
Sports, 74–77. *See also* Exercise
Statistics
    on average adult heights, 19
    on average growth rate, 18–20
    on children with growth prob-
        lems, 59
    on desired height, 11
    on long-range trends in growth
        rates, 51–52
    on pubertal age, 44

Tallest adult human, 33
Tallest human group, 27
Tallest living woman, 69
Tanner, Dr. James M., 45
Teasing, 79–82
Teenagers. *See* Adolescence
Testes. *See* Sex glands
Testosterone. *See* Sex hormones
Thyroid hormone, 33, 65
Tom Thumb, 31–32
Turner's syndrome, 62, 64

Villechaize, Herve, 30
Vitamins, 51. *See* Nutrition and
    diet
Voice
    changes in male, 40, 45
    impression of, 73

Watusis, 27
Webb, "Spud", 75